MW00891696

JOURNEY

- a traveler's notes -

–William Sulit and Beth Kephart –

INTRODUCTION

This illustrated journal opens the door to your dreams, your thoughts, your stories. Perhaps the angel dangling from strings reminds you of a cloud you once saw passing. Perhaps the boys in the boat float you back to an adventure. Perhaps the lady with the birds in a cluck upon her head is a version of your future self in the room that you will someday build. Where is that room? What color is your sky?

A handful of images. A handful of words. A lifetime of stories.

Anything you want to say, anything you want to draw, any color you wish to add—there's room for you here.

I might have cried, but for the moon and for the thought
of you tracing the places
we once had been, the person
I had promised you I'd be.

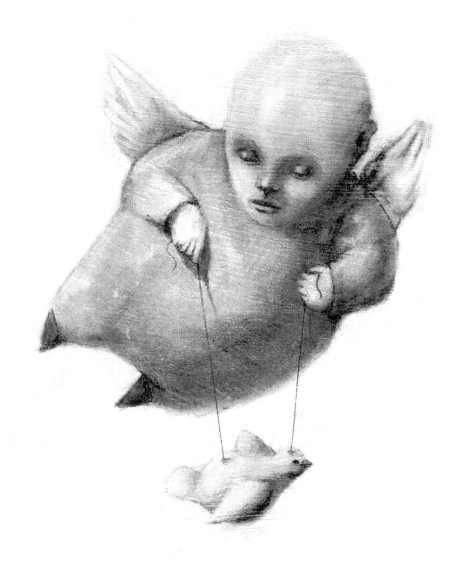

Wishing I had learned color instead of words.

Wings

In the same way that a stone wall falls
more sensationally than it stands,
in the same way that a rescued love
is made more tender by its damage,
in the same way that women understand beauty
only in its passing, you in the bar in Prague
blew smoke up through the crevices of language.
Smoke the color of angel wings.

Sometimes just a few white saucers will float down from the sky and I want to wake you. Snow, I might say. Open your eyes.

Yesterday I recognized a tenderness in you
accepting the small stuffed bear a child offered
for no one else's sake.

Beauty being in the bend of things and in the wide omnivorous

eye of a bloom.

I calculate figures of speech at dawn.
I write until I bless us both with losses.

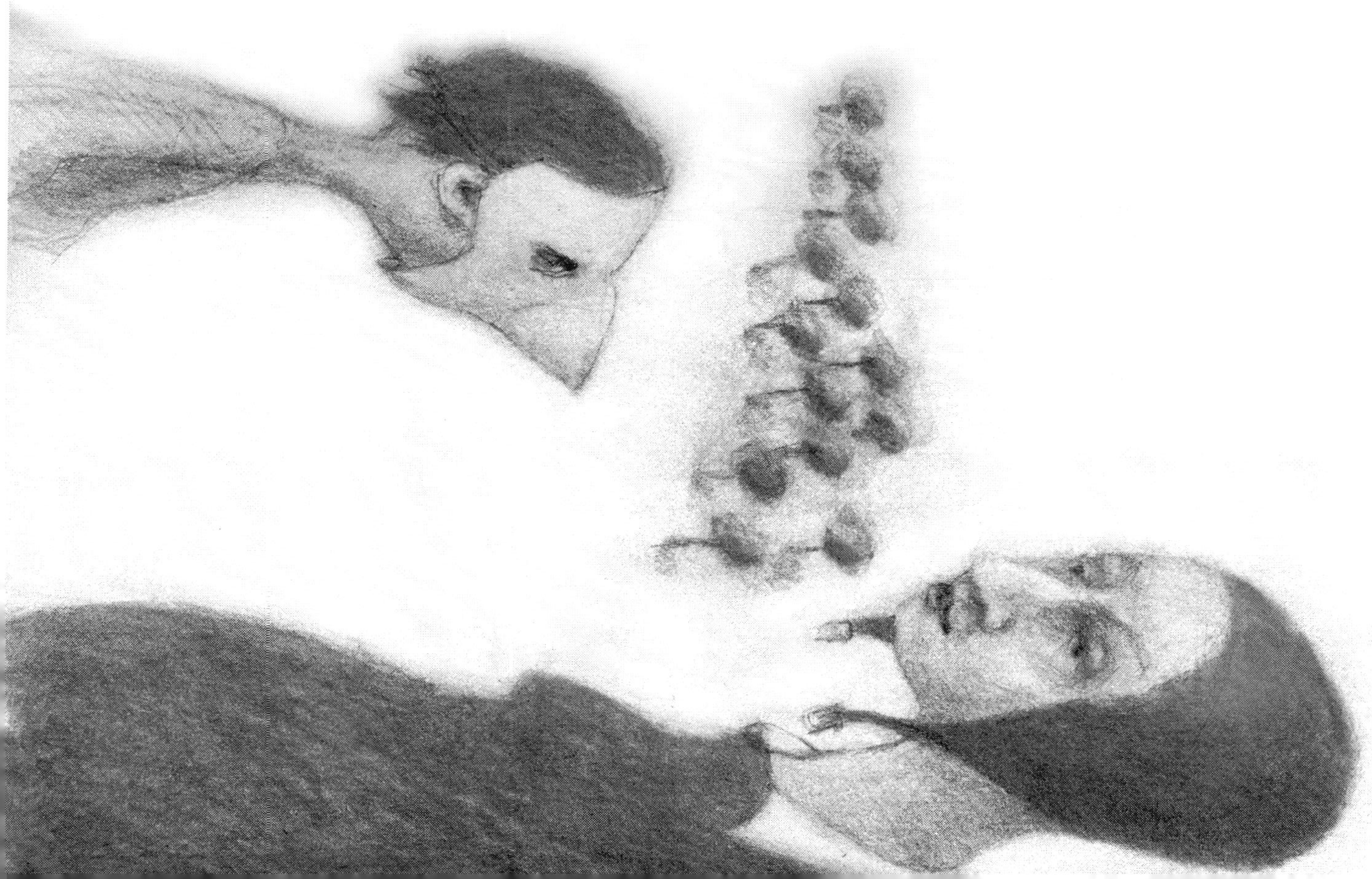

Afternoon, and the sky around the heart is blue.

I ran through rooms. I misappropriated my hair.

The first bird bleats. The second
calls through the wings that are caught
in its throat, so that it goes like that:
bleating and rustling,
then silence.

Desire

I want a room with a hole for a roof that telescopes the sky
and a floor of dirt that accepts the seeds that slip
between my fingers. I want a chair built of root and vine
and a table a bird might nest on, freckled eggs,
cyan in the contour of the shadows,
a long and necessarily white bed.

You could come to me in my room at night,
when our differences are less transparent,
when your idea of God could rest
with my idea of God, and in that way signify
the future. I would trade any poem for my room,
and you would watercolor with a feather,

and when the garden grew itself tall,
to the moon, we would have finally vanished.
It is enough to be still and to trust the owl
with every danger. It is enough
to anticipate the want of life
within the freckle of an egg.

I never touch a pearl to my ear without hearing you first.

Forecast

I will always want the whole moon
white where it is, blue how it falls.
I will always say, Bring me the peony,
and covet the smell of parsley
on the edge of a knife.

His voice loose and cool with that
conversion of regret
that is not merely ash and not combustion.

The distance between now and then is the ants, spilled

as if from a candy dish.

The chiaroscuro of wings launched into the still white hull of winter.

What is the color of the shadow on the snow?

Once, late at night on the street, when I should not have been alone, a cauldron of deer steamed apart to let me pass. The deer lanterned me home with their eyes.

Sometimes a bird sings in the language of memory,
and that is the start of a poem.

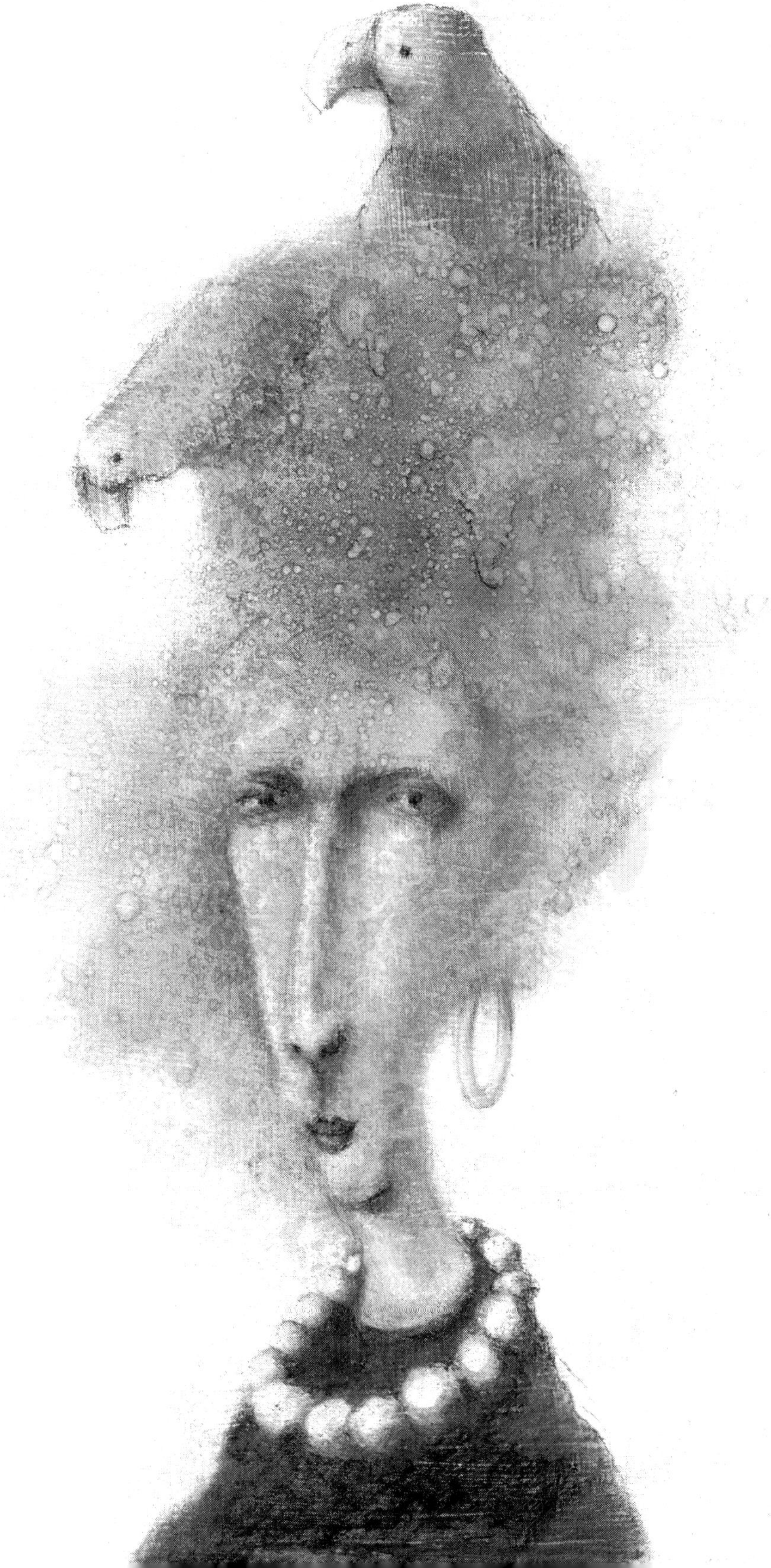

We are working with inversions, with stolen hips and wings.

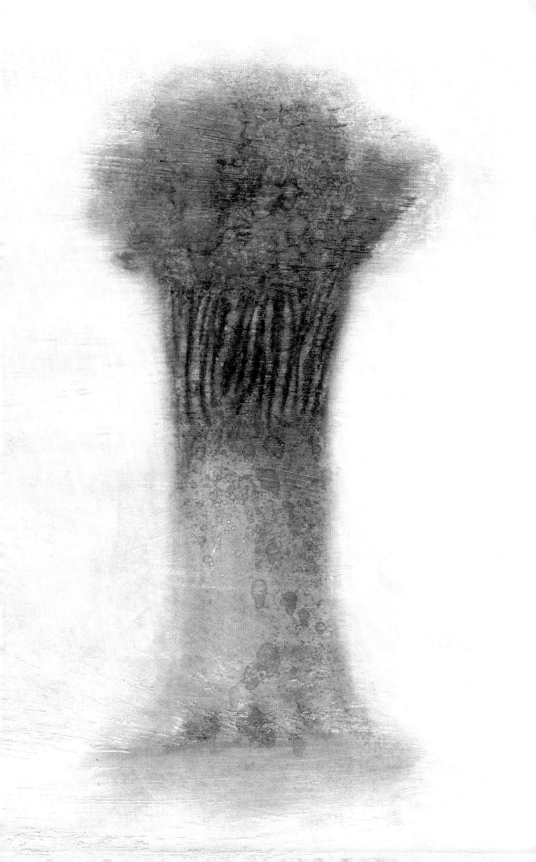

You never brought me the right presents on purpose.

In the white saucer of your car through the dark
we drove,
the water wide to our either side,
the earth collapsible and folding.

I stand in the rooms of the dead, listening
to the groan of the earth beneath the tree.

Before this you had been
standing on the falling down
part of the hill.
You had been laughing.
Twenty years, someone said,
and no one's changed.

We talked as neighbors do of fireflies and June bugs
and the elephant circus that had come to town.

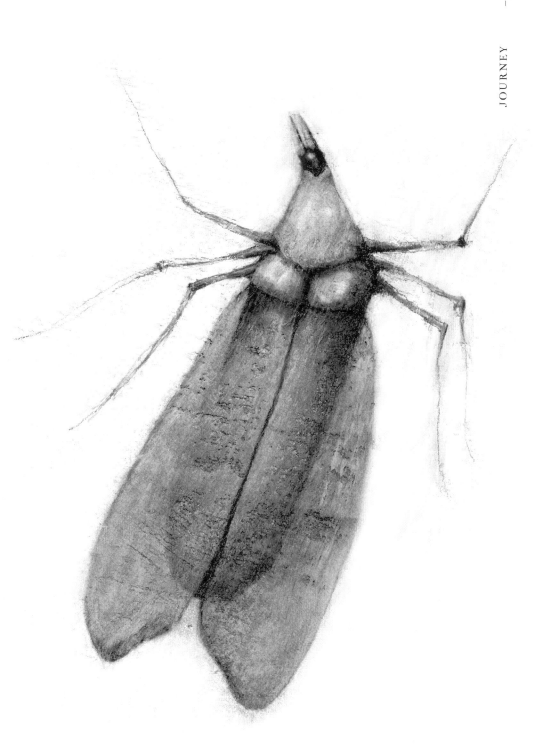

Excuse me, but do you remember
the day we found him
in a plastic bin of doll parts
beneath a rippling flea market tent
in Amish country beside a beer garden?

I tried to kiss you but you turned.

Living life

extravagantly in the margins.

She'd left three slips
drying on the line you could barely reach
if you almost fell through the kitchen window.
Also a peach on the table and the old bear
of her winter coat in the closet because it was still,
in some ways, an animal.

Walking the streets in the dark after a storm,
looking for life through the lit-up glass of other people's stories.

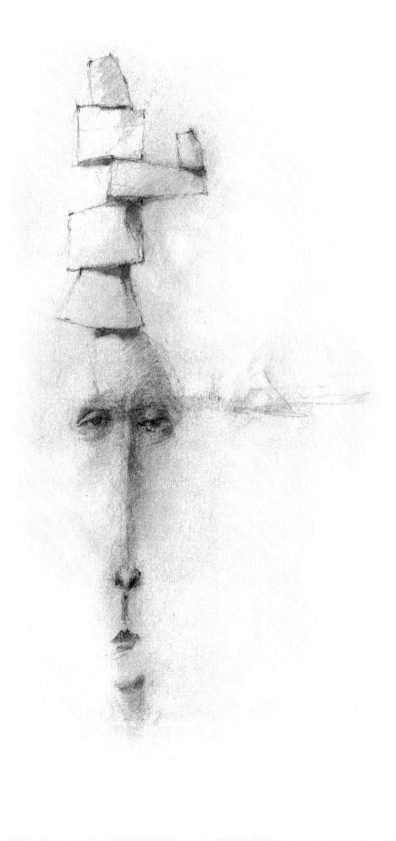

Later I carry two skulls home
in a suitcase of books.
I roost them
in my own dark cabinet of curiosities,
and live in search of the authentic:
A song not eclipsed by the hollow.
A poem as white as bone.

It had been what we'd taken for ourselves,
from a room of fragile things,
in a shop on the river on a day
when again it was the three of us,
and we were accumulating time
for after this.

We went to war with false pear trees and roses,
with oak leaf hydrangea, aster, phlox,
the irises we'd been loaned
by friends, the sweetened sugar
of the peonies.

That is my face, caught in the glass.

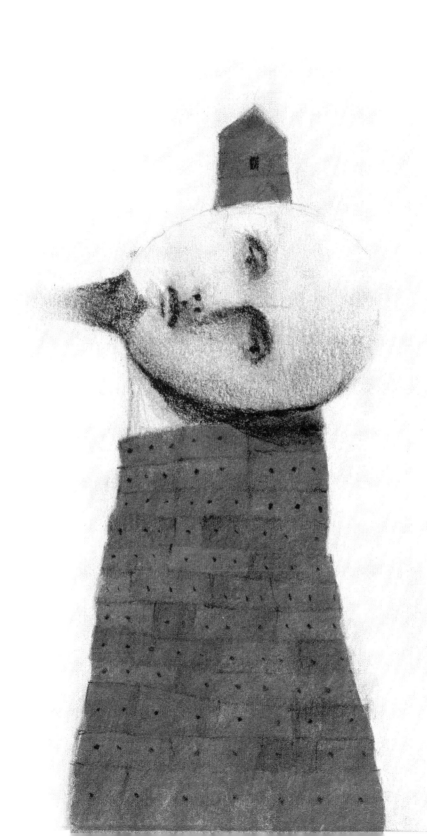

I settle the pain in my head by remembering
the butterfly I once drew
all the one day and then the next,
until its wings were a stained-glass firmament
and its antennae fuzzed the way antennae do.

Somewhere

there's a catastrophe with a trash can.

BIOGRAPHIES

William Sulit is an award-winning illustrator, ceramicist, and designer. Born in El Salvador, he studied design at North Carolina State and received his Masters of Architecture degree from Yale University. He is the co-founder of Juncture Workshops, offering memoir workshops, publications, and resources, and frequently collaborates with his wife, Beth, on book projects. Follow him on Instagram at @ws_studioarts.

Beth Kephart is the award-winning author of more than two-dozen books in multiple genres, an award-winning teacher at the University of Pennsylvania, a widely published essayist and critic, and co-founder of Juncture Workshops. Her collaborations with her husband, William, include illustrated memoirs, middle-grade novels, a corporate fable, and the memoir workbook, *Tell the Truth. Make It Matter.* More at bethkephartbooks.com.

Made in the USA
Middletown, DE
23 September 2019